Alfred's Basic Piano Library

Prep Course

FOR THE YOUNG BEGINNER

Willard A. Palmer · Morton Manus · Amanda Vick Lethco

Theory Book · Level E

INSTRUCTIONS FOR USE

1. This book is designed for use with Alfred's PREP COURSE for the YOUNG BEGINNER, LESSON BOOK E. The first assignment should be made when the student receives the Lesson Book.

2. As with all the supplementary books of this series, the pages of this THEORY BOOK are coordinated page by page with the LESSON BOOK. Pages 2 and 3 contain a game (Identify the U.F.O.'s) that reviews 17 important concepts that have been taught in earlier books. The book continues with pages that introduce the dotted quarter note, giving reinforcement to the very same concept that is introduced in the corresponding pages of the Lesson Book. When all assignments are made according to the instructions in the upper right corner of each page in the THEORY BOOK, adequate drill on each new concept is assured, along with continuing review of principles previously learned.

3. In this book, the student is drilled on harmonic and melodic intervals up to and including the octave, and continues to learn to move more freely and fluently over the keyboard. 2 over 1 is introduced before 3 over 1. Passing 1 under 2, 1 under 3, and 1 under 4 will be introduced later. This thoughtful approach carefully builds the hand of the young pianist, avoiding the development of poor playing habits, such as twisting the wrist when playing scale passages.

4. Because of the attractive games and puzzles included in this book, many students may wish to fill in these pages in advance of their assignments. While such eagerness is commendable, it is best for the student to wait until the indicated pages in the Lesson Book have been covered before the corresponding material in this book is completed.

5. Private students are usually expected to complete theory assignments at home with the written work checked at the beginning of each lesson or before the next assignment is made. In class teaching, theory assignments may be used as classroom drill, with most or all of the written work completed at the lesson.

Illustrations by Christine Finn   •   Music Engraving by Nancy Butler   •   Layout by Tom Gerou

Identify the U.F.O.'s!

The U.F.O's (Unidentified Flying Objects) on pages 2 and 3 can be changed to
I.F.O.'s (Identified Flying Objects)!

To change the U.F.O.'s to I.F.O.'s, print the name of each space ship on the tag attached to it.
Select from the following names:

QUARTER REST	SHARP	FORTE	TIED NOTES	TIME SIGNATURE
HALF REST	FLAT	MEZZO FORTE	ACCENT	REPEAT
WHOLE REST	NATURAL	PIANO	FERMATA	EIGHTH NOTES

Score 100 for each U.F.O. you identify! Perfect score is 1,500!

FOR BONUS SCORE, ANSWER THE FOLLOWING QUESTIONS
TO MAKE 1,700 AND QUALIFY AS A SUPER-STUDENT!

1. *p–mf* means _____ .

2. _____ means "gradually _____ ."

YOUR SCORE _____

Use with pages 6–7.

Dotted Quarter Notes

A DOT increases the length of a note by ONE HALF ITS VALUE.

2 counts   +   1 count   =   3 counts

1 count   +   ½ count   =   1½ counts

Here are two different ways of writing the same rhythm:

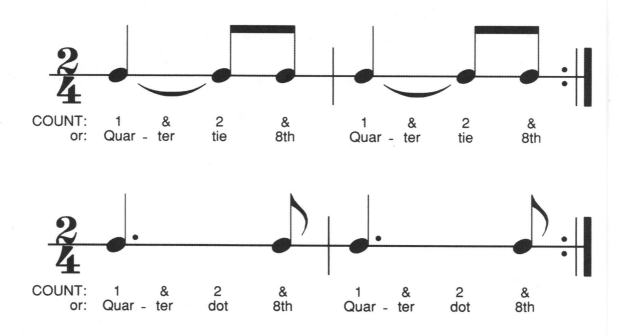

COUNT: 1   &   2   &   1   &   2   &
or: Quar - ter   tie   8th   Quar - ter   tie   8th

COUNT: 1   &   2   &   1   &   2   &
or: Quar - ter   dot   8th   Quar - ter   dot   8th

Count aloud and clap (or tap) the rhythm of the two examples above.

(Clap ONCE for each note.) Are the rhythms the same?_____

Dotted Quarter Notes in ¾ Time

1. In the following line, draw TIES as indicated.
2. Play and count.
3. Play and sing the words.

4. In the following line, some quarter notes need dots.
   Add the correct dots to make the rhythm the same as above.
5. Play and count. This line should sound *exactly* the same as the one above.

Dotted Quarter Notes in 4/4 Time

6. In the following line, draw TIES as indicated.
7. Play and count.
8. Play and sing the words.

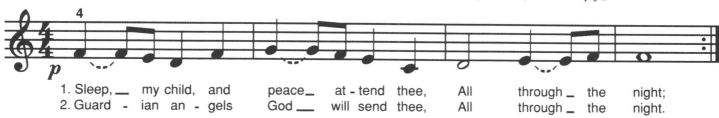

9. In the following line, there are some dots missing from quarter notes and some flags missing from eighth notes. Add everything that is needed to make the rhythm the same as above.
10. Play and count. This line should sound *exactly* the same as the one above.

IMPORTANT! In 2/4, 3/4, or 4/4 time, a **DOTTED QUARTER NOTE** is usually followed by an **EIGHTH NOTE!**

Use with page 8.

Rhythm Review

Draw lines connecting the dots on the boxes in which the total note values and rest values are the same in $\frac{4}{4}$ time.

NOTE VALUES　　　**REST VALUES**

Score 20 for each pair of boxes correctly connected.

PERFECT SCORE = 140　　　YOUR SCORE _____

The Streets of Laredo

1. Add the missing BAR LINES. Because this piece begins with an INCOMPLETE MEASURE, it must also end with an incomplete measure. Use a DOUBLE BAR at the end.

2. Add the missing RESTS for whichever hand is not playing.

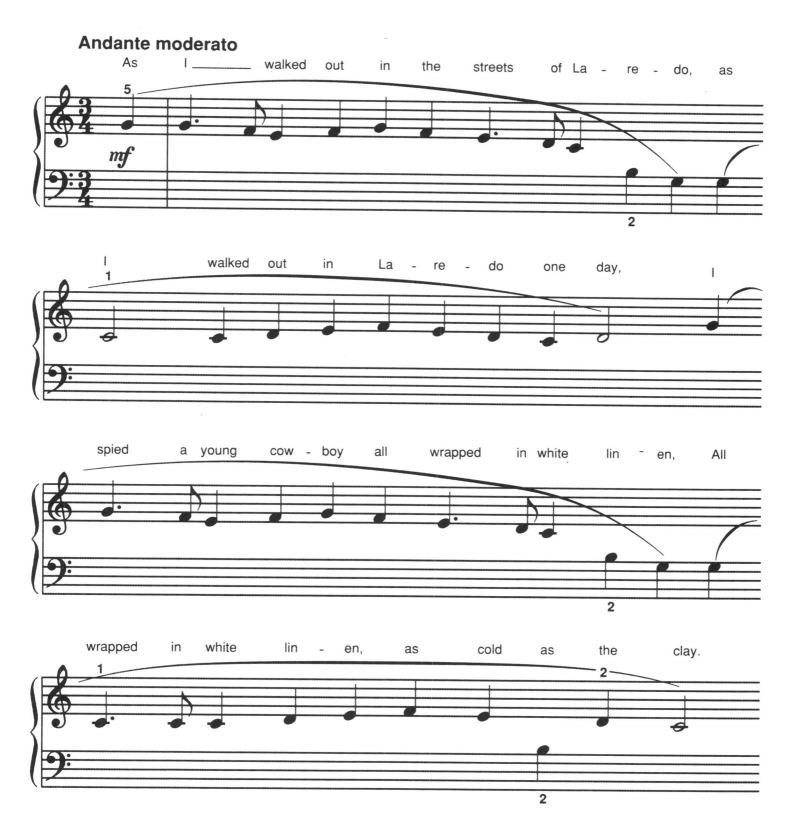

3. Play *THE STREETS OF LAREDO* slowly, counting aloud.

Use with page 10.

Time to Rap Again!

1. Say the words in rhythm while you tap your foot four times to each measure. Clap your hands on each rest. Snap your fingers on each note shaped like an X. Rap all pairs of eighth notes EVENLY.

2. When rapping with several people, you can "RAP a ROUND." After one person or one group raps the first two lines, another person or group can join in, starting from the beginning.

Allegro moderato

Now it's time to rap a - gain!

Time to rap and clap a - gain!

Ev - 'ry - bod - y rap! Ev - 'ry - bod - y clap!

Dot - ted rhy - thms are a snap!

Rap a - bout the things you like to do,

Play - ing the pi - an - o with a friend or two.

Ev - 'ry - bod - y rap! Ev - 'ry - bod - y clap!

Dot - ted rhy - thms are a snap!

Identify the Hand Positions

This is the first of several exercises in this book that will give you practice in moving from one 5-finger position to another. Each of these measures is in C POSITION or G POSITION.

1. Write a C or a G in each of the following boxes, to identify the position of each measure.

2. Play all of the above. Carefully observe dynamic signs, legato and staccato indications.

Use with page 12.

Measuring 6ths

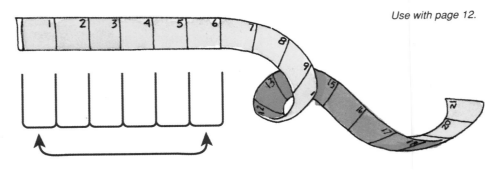

When you skip 4 white keys, the interval is a **6th**.

6ths are written LINE-SPACE or SPACE-LINE.

1. Write the name of each note in the following boxes.
2. Play these MELODIC INTERVALS, saying "Up a 6th," etc.

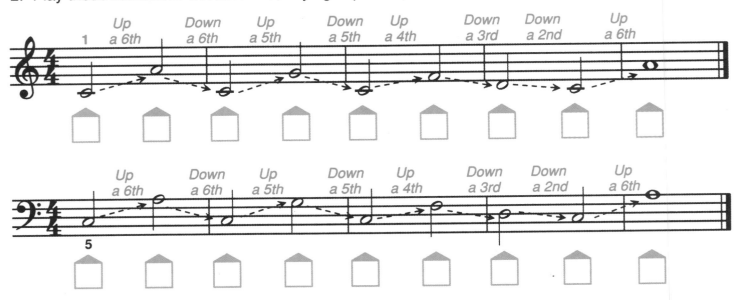

3. In each measure below, add a higher whole note to make the indicated HARMONIC INTERVAL, as shown in the first example.

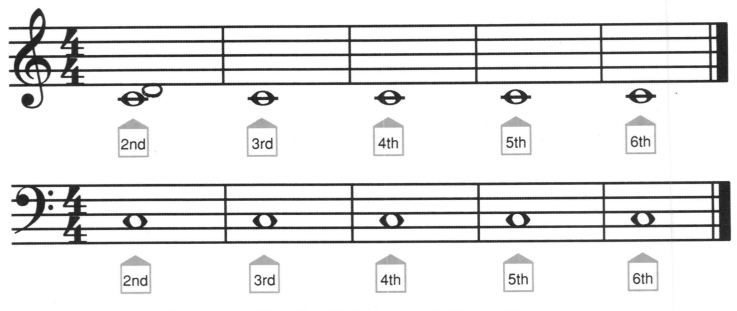

4. Play the above two lines. Use RH 1–5 or LH 5–1 on each 5th and 6th.

Interval Study

Use with page 13.

1. Write the name of each harmonic interval in the box above it. Use 5 for 5th, etc.
2. Play, saying the name of each interval.

REVIEW: Directing $\frac{3}{4}$ Time

3. Direct the following measures.
   Say or sing the words as you direct.
   Each beat of the baton must have exactly the same tempo!

Allegro moderato

mf

1. Lav - en - der's blue, dil - ly, dil - ly, Lav - en - der's green.
2. Who told you so, dil - ly, dil - ly, Who told you so?

When I am King, dil - ly, dil - ly, You shall be Queen!
'Twas my own heart, dil - ly, dil - ly, That told me so!

"Fire at Intervals!"

Draw a straight line from each Interval Shooter to touch any part of the balloon that carries the interval of the same name. Use a ruler or straight edge. The lines may cross, but may not pass through a different interval!

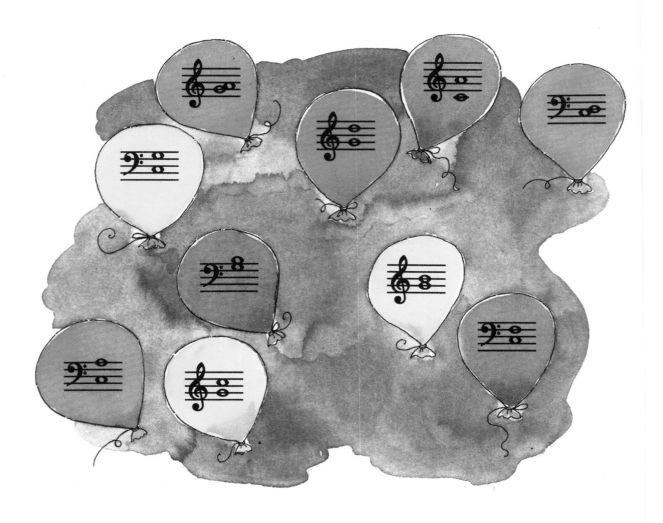

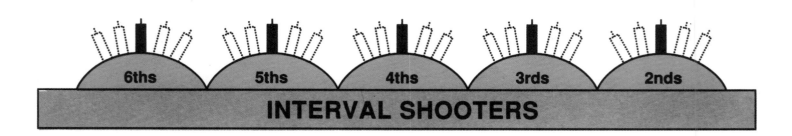

Score 10 for each interval shot down.

PERFECT SCORE = 100   YOUR SCORE _____

REVIEW: Directing 2/4 and 4/4 Time

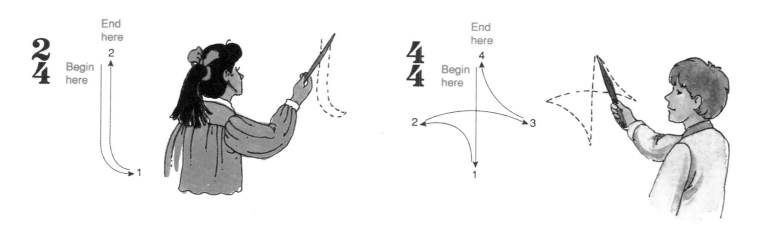

KUM-BA-YAH uses 2/4 and 4/4 time, changing the time signature in each measure.

Direct the following measures. Say or sing the words as you direct.
Each beat of the baton must be at exactly the same tempo!

14

Use with page 16.

6ths from B to G

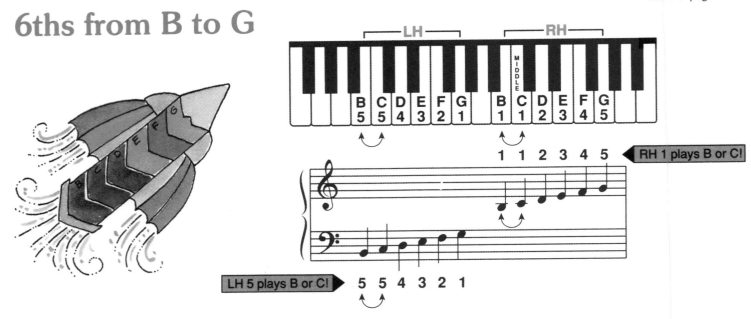

1. Write the name of each interval on this page in the box below it. Use 2 for 2nd, etc.

2. Play all the intervals on this page, saying the name of each as you play.

Conversation Piece

Use with page 17.

(Happy—Serious)

1. In measures 1 through 8, add a sign over or under each notehead, meaning PLAY STACCATO.
   If the stem points down, add the sign over the notehead.
   If the stem points up, add the sign under the notehead.
2. In measures 9 through 16, add one sign over or under all the notes of each measure, meaning PLAY LEGATO. Do not cross the bar lines.
3. Play.

Use with pages 18–19.

The "Music Cube"
(Note Reading Review)

Solve this cube by filling in the squares like a CROSS-WORD PUZZLE.

TOP

Across

1. The 2nd month.
   (Abbreviation)

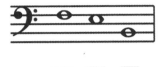

— — —

3. My "Pop."
   (Another nickname)

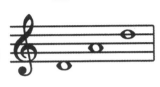

— — —

Down

1. A hungry cat likes
   to be this.
   (So does a dog.)

— — —

2. A good place
   to sleep.
   (Or grow flowers.)

— — —

Across

1. It means "to
   ask for."
   (My dog can
   do this.)

— — —

3. Just a little bit.
   (Also, "to pat.")

— — —

Down

1. Not good.
   (Don't be that way!)

— — —

2. It means
   "to talk a lot."
   (Or "a lot of talk.")

— — —

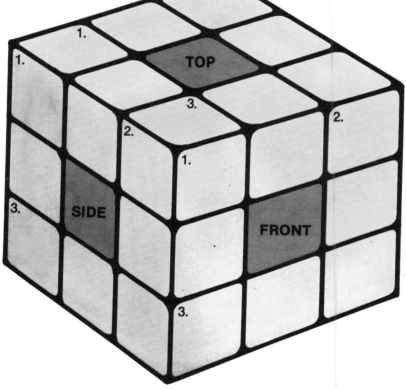

FRONT

Across

1. It can sting.
   (Or make sweet
   stuff.)

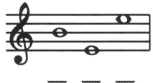

— — —

3. Talk too much and
   you may get one.
   (That's a joke!)

— — —

Down

1. Something's in it.
   (A sandwich,
   maybe?)

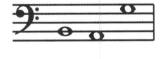

— — —

2. It's good in a
   scramble.
   (Or an omelette.)

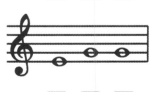

— — —

If you guessed the words from the clues, fill in the blanks under the notes anyway,
to test your note reading skill! Score 10 for each correct answer.

PERFECT SCORE = 120   YOUR SCORE _____

The Musical Private Eye

𝄾 1	*mp* 2	> 3	♯ 4
p 5	*Fine* 6	⟩ 7	*pp* 8
♭ 9	𝄐 10	♮ 11	⌐⌐ 12
𝄿 13	*mf* 14	< 15	**3/4** 16

In the squares below, write the numbers that identify each musical clue given above.

TIME SIGNATURE	**16**	☐	PIANISSIMO (very soft)
NATURAL SIGN	☐	☐	FERMATA (hold sign)
FLAT SIGN	☐	☐	DIMINUENDO (gradually softer)
SHARP SIGN	☐	☐	CRESCENDO (gradually louder)
QUARTER REST	☐	☐	PIANO (soft)
THE END	☐	☐	MEZZO PIANO (moderately soft)
EIGHTH REST	☐	☐	PEDAL SIGN
ACCENT MARK	☐	☐	MEZZO FORTE (moderately loud)

Add 10 points for each correct answer.

PERFECT SCORE = 160　　　　　YOUR SCORE _____

Use with pages 20–21.

Moving Up & Down the Keyboard in 6ths

1. Add a note a 6th ABOVE each of the following notes.
   Say the name of the note as you write it.

2. Play, using RH 1–5 on each 6th.

3. Add a note a 6th BELOW each of the following notes.
   Say the name of the note as you write it.

4. Play, using LH 5–1 on each 6th.

5. Play the two lines as one complete piece—play RH, then LH.

Moving Around the Keyboard in 6ths

1. Add a note a 6th ABOVE each of the following notes.
   Say the name of the note as you write it.

2. Play, using RH 1–5 on each 6th.

3. Add a note a 6th BELOW each of the following notes.
   Say the name of the note as you write it.

4. Play, using LH 5–1 on each 6th.

5. Play the two lines as one complete piece—play RH, then LH.

Modernly We Roll Along!
(Moving Up & Down the Keyboard in 3rds)

Use with page 22.

1. Add a note a 3rd BELOW each LH note except the last two notes of line 2 (G, C).
2. Play. Use the fingering 2–4 on each RH 3rd, and 4–2 on each LH 3rd.
   Notice that the 2nd fingers of the RH & LH are always playing a 2nd apart!
   Listen carefully to the modern sounds made by 3rds used in this manner.

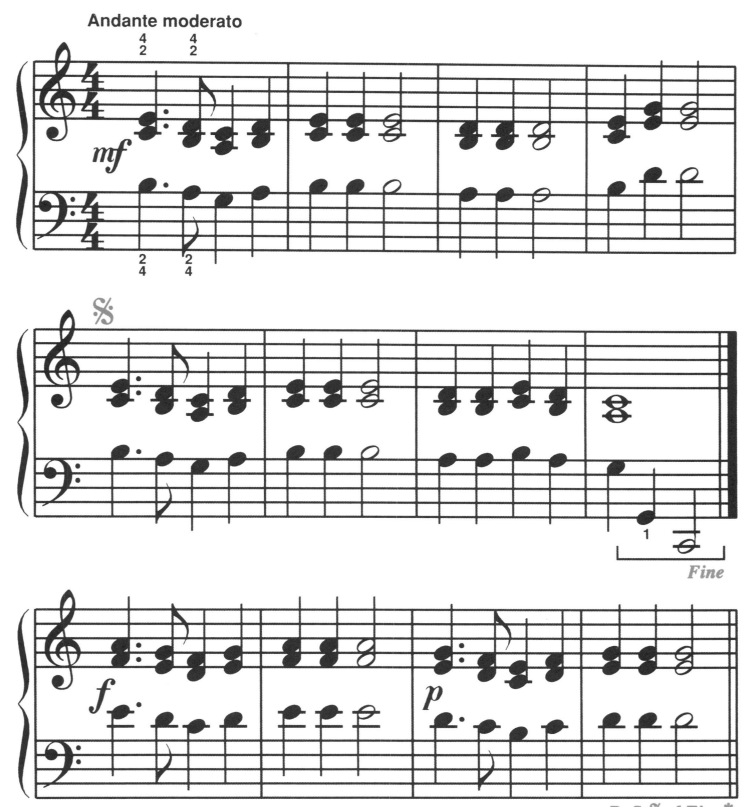

*D. S. % al Fine**

*Repeat from the sign % (see the beginning of the 2nd line) and play to the *Fine*.

20

Use with page 23.

Crossing LH 2 over 1
—A Fingering Trick!

You can play any 6 neighboring white keys in a row,
going UP the keyboard with the LH, by starting with
the 5th finger and crossing 2 over 1.

1. Write the finger number under each of the following notes, as shown in the first example.
   Use LH 5 4 3 2 1 2 1 for each ascending group of notes.
2. Write the names of the notes in the boxes.
3. Play.

Use with page 23.

Crossing RH 2 over 1
—A Fingering Trick!

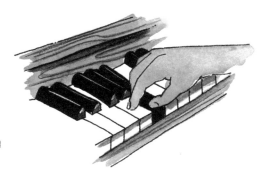

You can also play any 6 neighboring white keys in a row, coming DOWN the keyboard with the RH, by starting with the 5th finger and crossing 2 over 1.

1. Write the finger number over each of the following notes, as shown in the first example. Use RH 5 4 3 2 1 2 1 for each descending group of notes.
2. Write the names of the notes in the boxes.
3. Play.

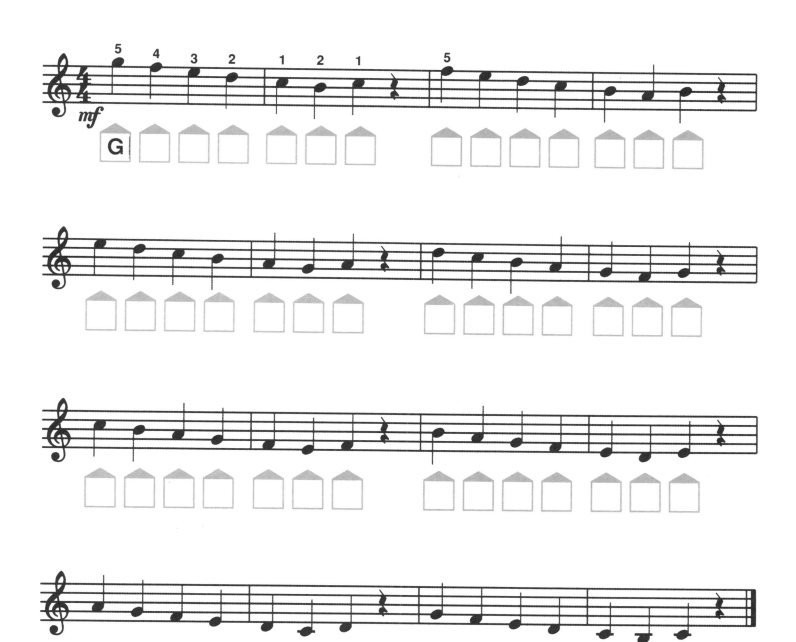

Use with page 25.

Figuring the Fingering

Now that you have learned the trick of crossing 2 over 1 and are becoming more skilled at moving to different positions on the keyboard, you can begin to choose your own fingering. Only the first finger for each line is given.

1. Fill in the squares with the best finger numbers for playing this piece. Notice that you do not have to finger every note. The second measure is exactly like the first; it is played with the same fingering.

2. Play the piece several times, using the fingering you wrote.

REVIEW: Six Dynamic Signs

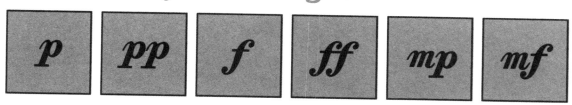

1. Each of the above dynamic signs has two matches below;
   one in the LEFT column and one in the RIGHT column.

   Draw each sign TWICE; once in a square in the LEFT column and
   once in a square in the RIGHT column.

☐	FORTE	VERY SOFT ☐
☐	MEZZO PIANO	LOUD ☐
☐	PIANO	MODERATELY SOFT ☐
☐	FORTISSIMO	MODERATELY LOUD ☐
☐	MEZZO FORTE	SOFT ☐
☐	PIANISSIMO	VERY LOUD ☐

2. In the boxes below, write the six dynamic signs in increasing order of loudness,
   beginning with the softest one.

   ☐ ☐ ☐ ☐ ☐ ☐

3. In the boxes below, write the six dynamic signs in decreasing order of loudness,
   beginning with the loudest one.

   ☐ ☐ ☐ ☐ ☐ ☐

Score 5 for each box correctly filled.

PERFECT SCORE = 120   YOUR SCORE _____

24

Use with page 28.

Measuring 7ths

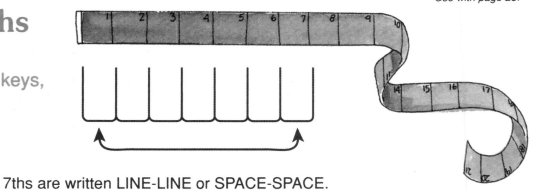

When you skip 5 white keys,
the interval is a **7th**.

7ths are written LINE-LINE or SPACE-SPACE.

UP a 7th   *DOWN a 7th*   *UP a 7th*   *DOWN a 7th*

1. In each measure below, add a higher half note to make the indicated MELODIC interval.

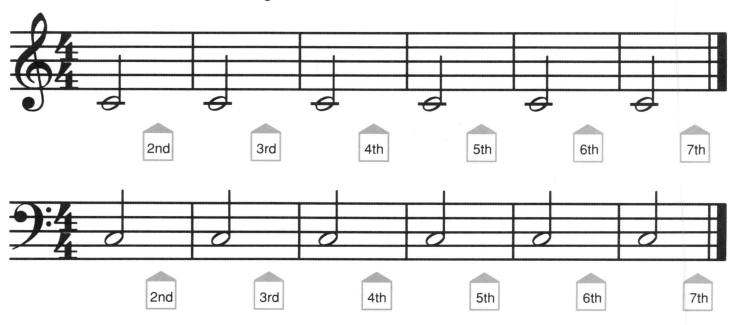

2nd 3rd 4th 5th 6th 7th

2nd 3rd 4th 5th 6th 7th

2. Play the above two lines. Use RH 1–5 or LH 5–1 on the 5th, 6th & 7th.

3. Above each of the following notes write another whole note to make a HARMONIC 7th,
   as shown in the first example.

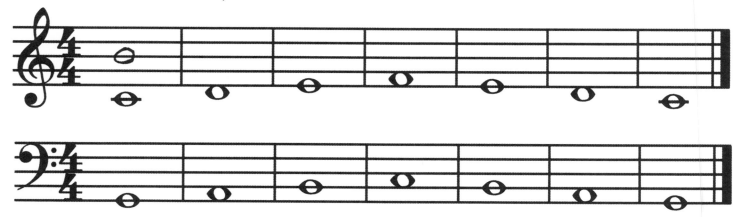

4. Play. Use RH 1–5 or LH 5–1 on each 7th.
   Students with hands too small to reach a 7th may divide each of the above lines between
   the hands, playing the bottom notes of the 7ths with LH 3, and the top notes with RH 3.

"Lucky Seven" Polka

1. In the music below, circle each pair of notes that make a MELODIC 7th.

2. How many harmonic 2nds can you find?   *(Answer)*_____

3. How many harmonic 3rds?_____

4. Harmonic 4ths?_____

5. Harmonic 5ths?_____

6. Harmonic 6ths?_____

7. Harmonic 7ths?_____

Use with page 32.

Crossing 3 over 1
to play the C Major Scale

1. Write the letter names of the notes of the C MAJOR SCALE, from *left* to *right*, on the keyboard below. Check each one with the TETRACHORD PATTERN as you write, to be sure the WHOLE STEPS & HALF STEPS are correct!

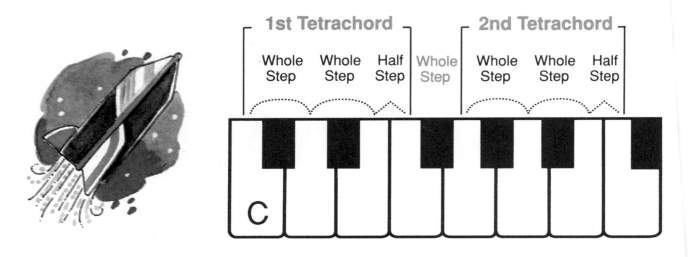

2. Complete the tetrachord beginning on C. Write one note over each finger number.

3. Complete the tetrachord beginning on G. Write one note over each finger number.

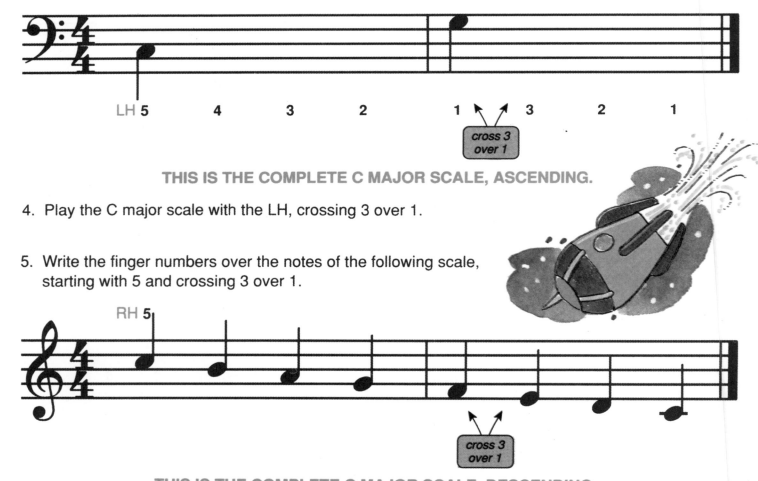

LH **5**   **4**   **3**   **2**   **1**   **3**   **2**   **1**

cross 3 over 1

THIS IS THE COMPLETE C MAJOR SCALE, ASCENDING.

4. Play the C major scale with the LH, crossing 3 over 1.

5. Write the finger numbers over the notes of the following scale, starting with 5 and crossing 3 over 1.

RH **5**

cross 3 over 1

THIS IS THE COMPLETE C MAJOR SCALE, DESCENDING.

6. Play the C major scale with the RH, crossing 3 over 1.

Opposites Attract!

Music is made more attractive by combining things that are opposite.
Draw a line connecting the dots on the boxes that contain opposites, as shown in the first example.

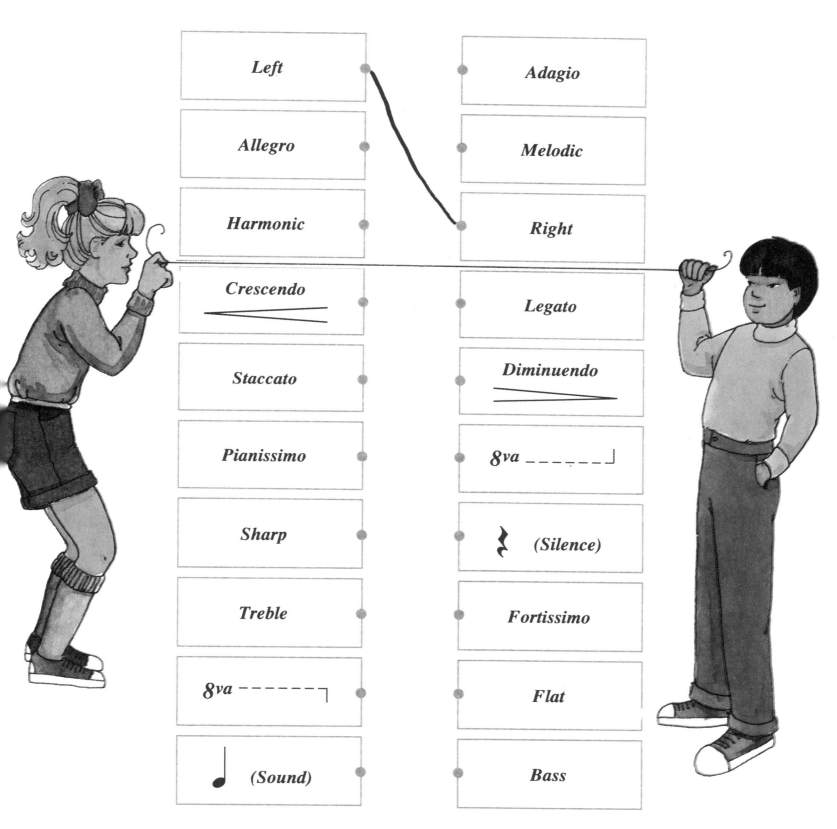

Score 10 for each pair of opposites correctly connected.

PERFECT SCORE = 100   YOUR SCORE _____

Use with page 36.

Measuring Octaves

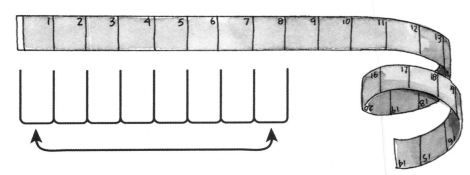

When you skip 6 white keys,
the interval is an **OCTAVE**.

Octaves are written LINE-SPACE or SPACE-LINE.

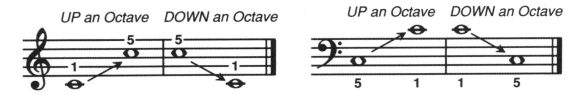

1. In each measure below, add a higher half note to make the indicated MELODIC interval.

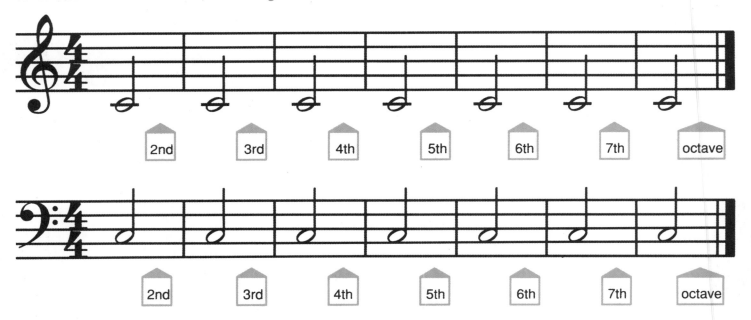

2. Play the above 2 lines. Use RH 1–5 or LH 5–1 on the 5th, 6th, 7th & octave.

3. Above each of the following notes write another whole note to make a HARMONIC OCTAVE, as shown in the first example.

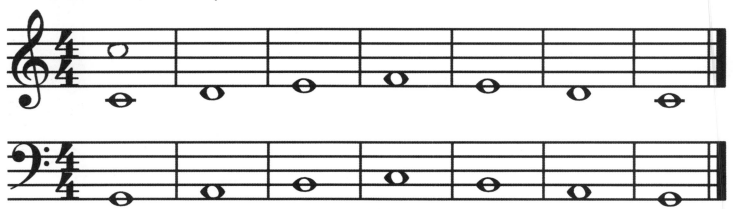

4. Play. Use RH 1–5 or LH 5–1 on each octave.
    Students with hands too small to reach an octave may divide each of the above lines between the hands, playing the bottom notes of the octaves with LH 3, and the top notes with RH 3.

Tips on Speed-Reading Intervals

Use with pages 38–39.

EVEN numbered intervals—2nds, 4ths, 6ths, octaves (8ths)—
have notes on LINE-SPACE or SPACE-LINE.

2nd   4ths   6ths   Octaves

ODD numbered intervals—3rds, 5ths, 7ths—
have notes on LINE-LINE or SPACE-SPACE.

3rds   5ths   7ths

See how quickly you can write the name of each interval in the box below it.
Use "2" for 2nd, etc., and "8" for OCTAVE.

EVEN NUMBERS (2nds, 4ths, 6ths, octaves):

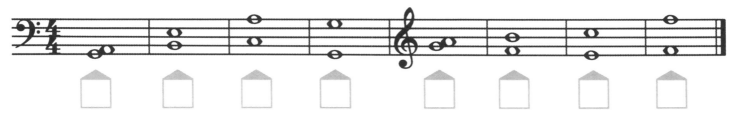

ODD NUMBERS (3rds, 5ths, 7ths):

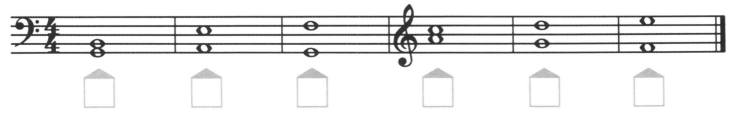

EVENS & ODDS:

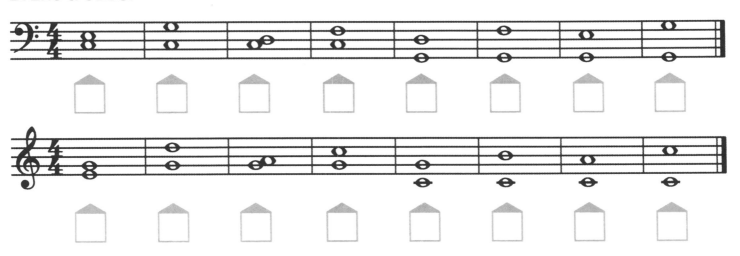

30

Use with page 40.

Crossing 3 over 1
to play the G Major Scale

1. Write the letter names of the notes of the G MAJOR SCALE, from *left* to *right,* on the keyboard below. Check each one with the TETRACHORD PATTERN as you write, to be sure the WHOLE STEPS & HALF STEPS are correct!

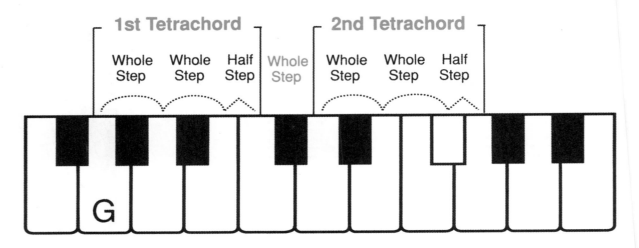

2. Complete the tetrachord beginning on G. Write one note over each finger number.

3. Complete the tetrachord beginning on D. Write one note over each finger number.

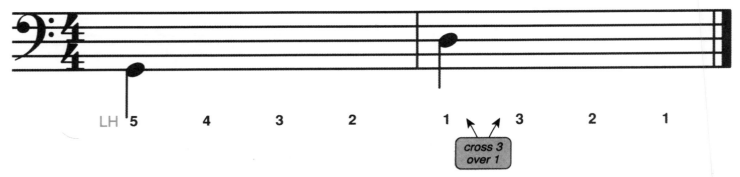

THIS IS THE COMPLETE G MAJOR SCALE, ASCENDING.

4. Play the G major scale with the LH, crossing 3 over 1.

5. Write the finger numbers over the notes of the following scale, starting with 5 and crossing 3 over 1.

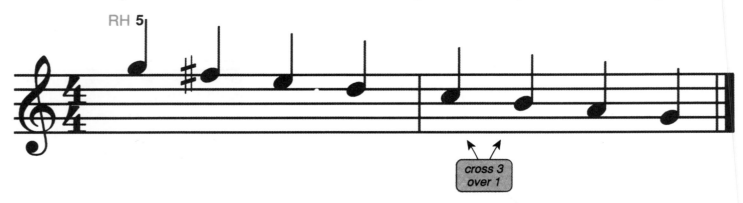

THIS IS THE COMPLETE G MAJOR SCALE, DESCENDING.

6. Play the G major scale with the RH, crossing 3 over 1.

"A-Maze-In" Intervals

This MAZE has 7 chambers, each containing a magic interval. Using a pencil, enter the maze at the top and trace a line to the chamber containing a 2nd. You must enter the chamber through the door with the arrow pointing INTO the chamber. Proceed around the interval and exit through the door with the arrow pointing OUT of the chamber. Proceed on to the chambers containing the 3rd, 4th, 5th, 6th, 7th & octave, in that specific order, then exit at the bottom of the maze. DO NOT CROSS ANY LINES YOU DRAW, and DO NOT USE THE SAME PATHWAY TWICE.

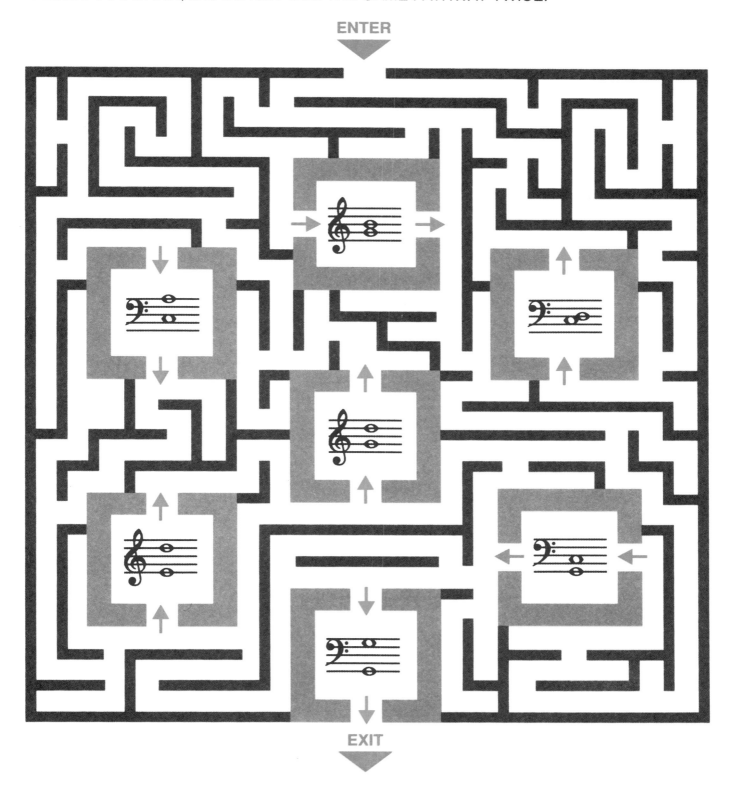

Now that you have found all the intervals in the maze, you are awarded the title M.A.G.I.C. (Marvelous and Great Interval Comprehender).

Reviewing the Grand Staff

Use with pages 44–45.

This page reviews all of the notes you have learned in levels A, B, C, D & E.

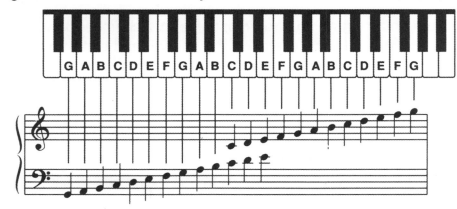

Some students use the following "memory aids" to help remember the names of the lines and spaces:

TREBLE CLEF *Lines:* "**E**very **G**ood **B**oy **D**oes **F**ine." *Spaces:* "**F A C E**."

BASS CLEF *Lines:* "**G**ood **B**oys **D**o **F**ine **A**lways." *Spaces:* "**A**ll **C**ows **E**at **Gr**ass."

If you have completed all of the pages in the Lesson Books and Theory Books that have gone before, you will instantly recognize all of the notes below without using the above "aids," which really slow down your note-reading. The best readers recognize individual notes instantly, but read by INTERVAL from note to note. Once the basic position is established, it isn't necessary to think of the name of each individual note.

1. These notes are on **LINES**. Write the names in the boxes.

2. These notes are in **SPACES**. Write the names in the boxes.

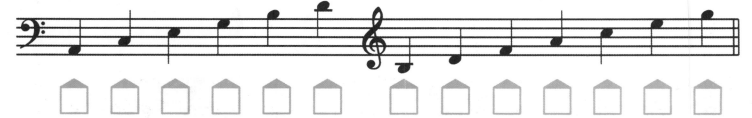

3. These notes are on **LINES & SPACES**. Write the names in the boxes.

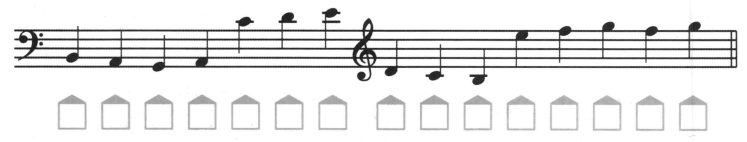